Discover the
Vikings

Warriors, Exploration and Trade

John C. Miles

W

FRANKLIN WATTS

LONDON·SYDNEY

Franklin Watts
First published in Great Britain in 2016 by The Watts Publishing Group

Credits
Series Editor: Amy Stephenson
Series Designer: Jane Hawkins
Picture Researcher: Diana Morris

Picture credits: All Canada Photos/Alamy: 25bl. Anielius/Shutterstock: front cover t. Anna/Dreamstime: 14b. The Art Archive/Alamy: 26c. Atlaspix/Shutterstock: 4b. Awe Inspiring Images/Shutterstock: 19bl. Kristof Bellens/ Dreamstime: 29tl. Alexandr Blinov/Dreamstime: 22c. CM Dixon/Getty Images: 8b. Donatas1205/Shutterstock: front cover b, 1t. Christian Fletcher. christianfletcher.com: 12br. Werner Forman Archive: 23t, 29cr. gezmen/Alamy: 23b. Jim Gibson/Alamy: 6b. Hel080808/Dreamstime: 25t. Historika Museet Stockholm/Leemage/BAL: 12bl. Doug Houghton/Alamy: 27t. hurstwic.com/13t. Lennart Larsen. CC-BY-SA National Museum, Denmark. http://samlinger. natmus.dk/DO/2094/ 4t, 5t, 6t, 7c, 8t, 9c, 10t, 10b, 12t, 13b, 14t, 15b, 16t, 17bl, 18t, 19br, 20t, 21cl, 22t, 23c, 24t, 25br, 26t, 27br, 28t, 28bl. Thue C. Leibrandt/CC Wikimedia: 20c. Olivier Le Queinec/Shutterstock: front cover bg. llliiioiiilll/ Shutterstock: front cover bg. David Muenker/Alamy: 21lt. Museum of London: front cover main, 15t, 17br. National Historical Museum, Stockholm/WHA/Superstock: 5b. Photogènes: 19t. Rigamondis/Dreamstime: 24b. Natalia Rumyantseva Dreamstime: 27bl. Jason Salmon/Shutterstock: 16c. Nikolai Sorokin/Dreamstime: 9b. Richard Tailby Derby Museums: 21br. Tt/Dreamstime: 1b, 11b. Marit S. Vea: 7b. The Viking Ship Society, Sebbe Als, Augustenborg: 10c. CC. wikimedia commons: 17t, 28br. wjarek/Shutterstock: 18b. Anna Yakimova/Dreamstime: 11t.

HB ISBN 978 1 4451 4886 1
PB ISBN 978 1 4451 5369 8

Printed in China

Franklin Watts
An imprint of
Hachette Children's Group
Part of The Watts Publishing Group
Carmelite House
50 Victoria Embankment
London EC4Y 0DZ

An Hachette UK Company
www.hachette.co.uk

www.franklinwatts.co.uk

Contents

Who were the Vikings?

Hundreds of years ago, around CE 800, bands of fierce warriors began raiding and looting in Europe. Many arrived by boat and became feared for their ruthless and deadly attacks. These warlike people became known as Vikings, which means 'sea pirate'. Although fighting and warfare were very important to them, Vikings were so much more than brutal monsters.

▼ Vikings came from the Scandinavian lands of Norway, Denmark and Sweden.

NORWAY

SWEDEN

DENMARK

Explorers

Viking seafarers set off on some of the most amazing voyages in the history of exploration. They were expert at finding their way across rough, open seas. Their sailing skills meant that they could successfully transport settlers to new lands.

Traders and merchants

Viking traders and merchants journeyed far and wide, selling objects from their homelands. They brought home exotic items made in distant places.

Farmers and settlers

Many Vikings lived in farming communities, raising crops and animals. Over time, Vikings conquered some of the lands they had raided and began to farm and build towns there too.

Craftworkers

At home, Viking craftworkers made beautiful objects in bone, wood and precious metal. Viking shipbuilders crafted vessels able to withstand battles or rough seas and sail up shallow rivers on trading and raiding voyages.

▲ This carved head from Sigtuna in Sweden depicts a Viking warrior. It was made out of elk horn in the 11th century.

Warriors and Viking society

At the top of Viking society were fearsome chieftains, each with his own band of warriors. Chieftains held power in their local areas.

A re-enactor dressed as a Viking warrior, complete with helmet, shield and sword. ▼

Power grabbing

At the beginning of the Viking period, around CE 600-700, Scandinavian countries were ruled by many of these local warlords. However, as time passed, the more ruthless chieftains defeated their neighbours and took their lands. By about 1050 a single king ruled each country.

IF YOU WERE A VIKING WARRIOR ...

If you fell out with someone you might choose to settle your differences by fighting an armed duel with swords or axes. A duel usually took place on a large piece of cloth. If you were forced by your opponent to step off the cloth, you lost the duel. If you forced him to step off the cloth, you won.

Rewards

Viking warriors expected to be well rewarded for their loyalty. If the chieftain they served didn't give them enough land and treasure, they left him to serve someone else who promised better rewards.

Elite group

An elite group of warriors, the 'Lith', lived with the chieftain. They acted as his bodyguards and retainers, and were ready to fight and die for him.

Disputes and feuds

Vikings settled disputes and made laws at a meeting of Vikings called a Thing. There were both local Things and larger regional ones, and a Thing usually lasted for several days. Wrongs between Viking families didn't go unpunished. If someone was murdered, the killer and his family had to pay 'blood money' to the victim's family. Feuds could simmer for generations.

WARRIORS AND OTHERS

As well as warriors, Viking society consisted of farmers, merchants and craftsmen. These were all *freemen*. Peasants without any land and thralls (slaves) worked for the freemen.

A modern re-enactment of Vikings travelling to a Thing in Iceland. ▼

Raiding, plunder and slaves

Towards the end of the 700s, Viking warriors left their homelands and began to attack Britain and other European countries. They were looking for treasure, slaves and, eventually, land to settle.

Vikings raid Britain

In 793 Vikings attacked the Christian Anglo-Saxon monastery of Lindisfarne, in the north of England. This was the first Viking raid on Britain. Monasteries such as Lindisfarne were undefended and contained valuable treasures made of gold, silver and jewels. The Vikings, who were not Christian, killed

▲ This carved gravestone from Lindisfarne dates from the 800s and shows armed Viking raiders.

the monks, stole the treasure and destroyed the monastery buildings. They attacked nearby villages and took local people home as slaves.

WHY DID VIKINGS GO RAIDING?

Farming was part of the Viking way of life. But farming was difficult in Scandinavian countries. Norway and Sweden are mountainous, with the best land in strips near the sea, and the soil is poor in parts of Denmark. So when populations grew it was hard to make a living. Seafaring Vikings probably set off in their ships to trade, but found raiding easier and more rewarding.

This photo of a Norwegian fjord, or sea inlet, demonstrates how little land was available for farming in many of the Viking homelands. ▼

Settling

As time went on, Vikings became less interested in raiding and were keen to live in the lands they had conquered. Once an area had been seized by warriors, settlers could then move in to farm and build towns.

Colonies

Land-hungry Vikings set up colonies in areas far from home, such as the Shetland Islands and Orkney Islands to the north of Scotland, and northern France. They settled there, traded, and sometimes fought with locals. Some settlements survived and were successful; others were abandoned.

Longships

Vikings were expert sailors. Their beautifully crafted ships carried bands of warriors on epic voyages over some of the most challenging seas in the world.

▲ A reconstruction of a Viking longship.

STEERING

Longships were steered by a helmsman using a single large oar on the right side. From this comes the term starboard ('steer-board') for the right-hand side of a ship.

Longships

Vikings used longships for both warfare and voyages of trading and exploration. A longship was up to 35 m long and could carry hundreds of warriors. It had one large square sail to catch the wind and oars for rowing. Longships were completely open, so a big piece of cloth stretched above the deck offered the only protection from the weather.

Fast and flexible

Longship hulls were slim, allowing them to slice through the water. They were made of wooden planks fastened with nails or wooden pegs and were 'clinker built', which meant that the planks overlapped. This way of building a ship allowed it to flex in rough seas and not be damaged. Gaps between the planks were sealed with tarred rope.

Longship hulls were shallow so that Vikings could sail close to coastlines and up river estuaries in search of plunder. Sailing close to a coastline was also safer than trying to navigate across large stretches of open ocean.

Figurehead

Viking longships often had a figurehead at the bow (front). This could be beautifully carved in the shape of a dragon or some other mythical beast.

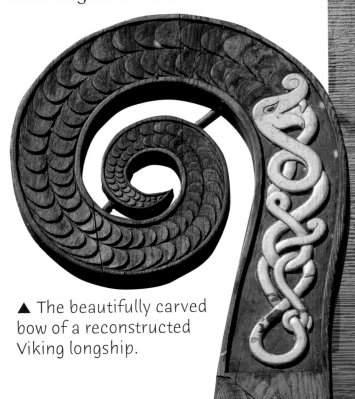

▲ The beautifully carved bow of a reconstructed Viking longship.

Viking swords

A Viking warrior's most prized possession was his sword. Swords were highly valuable weapons that were handed down from father to son.

Archaeologists have unearthed many Viking swords such as these. ▼

Names

Viking warriors gave their swords names, such as 'leg-biter' and 'snake of wounds', reflecting what the warriors believed the character of each weapon to be.

A rare weapon

Swords were made by skilled swordsmiths. As a result, they were rare and expensive objects. Of more than 100 Viking-era weapons found in graves in Iceland, only 16 are swords.

Modern replica Viking swords are crafted with the decorated features of the originals. ▼

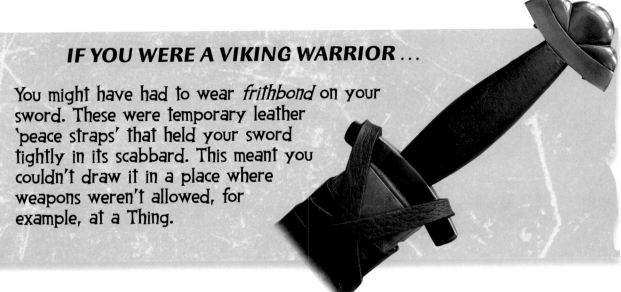

IF YOU WERE A VIKING WARRIOR ...

You might have had to wear *frithbond* on your sword. These were temporary leather 'peace straps' that held your sword tightly in its scabbard. This meant you couldn't draw it in a place where weapons weren't allowed, for example, at a Thing.

Making a sword

Early Viking-era swords were made by 'pattern-welding'. Several iron billets (blocks) were clamped together and heated in a furnace until they were white hot. Then the smith began to hammer them together into one piece of iron on an anvil (block of metal).

The smith repeatedly heated, turned and hammered the billets until they formed a long blade shape. This took a long time and required great strength. It was also very hot work.

When the blade was the right size and shape, it could be edged and sharpened. The pommel (the knob at the grip end) was added and the grip was covered with wood.

Brilliant blades

Most Viking swords were double edged, which means that both sides of the blade were sharpened. A typical sword was 60-90 cm long, weighed about 1-2 kg and had a slightly rounded point.

SCABBARD

A cover called a scabbard protected a Viking warrior's sword. It was made of three layers: an inner layer of wool, whose natural oil protected the blade from rust, then wood to stiffen the scabbard, and finally an outer covering of leather.

13

Armour, clothing and other weapons

What a Viking warrior wore into battle depended on how wealthy he was. Most Vikings went into battle wearing their everyday clothes.

▲ This Viking re-enactor wears a protective shirt of chain mail.

Chain mail

For a wealthy Viking chieftain, a shirt made of chain mail protected him in battles as well as showing his high status. The shirt was made from hundreds of interlocking iron rings that protected the wearer from slashing sword or axe cuts. Making chain mail was a skilled trade. Each shirt took a long time to make and cost a lot of money.

Helmet

Viking helmets were made of metal or leather reinforced with

IF YOU WERE A VIKING WARRIOR ...

Your ordinary clothes would consist of a long woollen tunic reaching to your knees, a pair of trousers or hose (woollen leggings) and sturdy leather shoes or boots. A thick cloak on top protected you from the cold. This was held in place by a decorated pin on one shoulder.

These Viking axe heads and spearheads were found in the River Thames in London. ▶

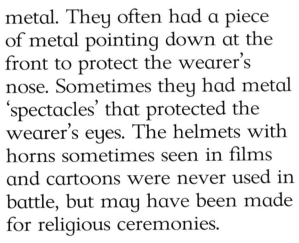
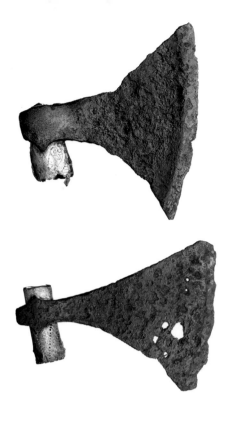

metal. They often had a piece of metal pointing down at the front to protect the wearer's nose. Sometimes they had metal 'spectacles' that protected the wearer's eyes. The helmets with horns sometimes seen in films and cartoons were never used in battle, but may have been made for religious ceremonies.

Axe

Although a sword (see pages 12-13) was the Viking warrior's most prized weapon, Vikings also used axes to smash through helmets in battle. They could be one- or two-handed, depending on the length of the shaft. The axe blade was sharp-edged, and lethal.

SHIELD

Shields were made from thick wood, covered with leather. Sometimes they had an iron rim. The warrior gripped a leather-covered handle on the back of the shield. A metal boss on the front protected the wearer's hand behind. Shields were painted with colourful patterns to identify those who carried them in the heat of battle.

Fighting on water

Longships made excellent warships. They were fast, manoeuvrable and could carry lots of warriors. Vikings used them in bloody naval battles or rowed them up river estuaries to attack targets, such as wealthy towns or monasteries.

▼ The shallow hulls of longships allowed Vikings to land raiders in tidal creeks, such as this one in eastern England.

Fjord feuds

These long, narrow sea inlets were good sites for battles between rival groups of feuding Vikings, as the waters of a fjord were calmer than the open ocean and there was less chance of an enemy escaping. Longships could be rowed at speed to ram an enemy vessel or lashed together to form a fighting platform for hand-to-hand combat. They could also be used to launch a storm of arrows at an enemy.

Battle of Svolder

This sea battle took place in CE 1000. A Viking story describes how King Olaf Tryggvason was surrounded by enemies on his ship, the *Long Serpent*. Caught in a hail of arrows, Olaf's men tried to board the enemy vessels, but fell in the gaps between them and drowned. Finally, surrounded, Olaf himself jumped overboard rather than allow himself to be taken prisoner.

▲ A page from the medieval Icelandic manuscript *Heimskringla*, which gives an account of the Battle of Svolder.

ATTACKS ON LONDON

Wealthy London, still protected by its Roman walls, was attacked several times by Viking warriors, starting in about 830. The raid in 842 was known as 'the great slaughter', and in 851 as many as 350 Viking ships attacked the city. In 994, Danish Vikings led by Sweyn Forkbeard sailed up the River Thames and tried to burn London but were defeated. Finally, in 1016, London fell under the control of Danish King Cnut.

This decorated Viking sword belt dates from the early 1000s and is in the Museum of London, along with other Viking artefacts from the time of King Cnut. ▶

17

Battle tactics

Viking warriors mainly fought on foot. A battle began with shouted insults and a hail of arrows and spears. The two sides then advanced for bloody hand-to-hand combat.

Under the raven banner

The raven is a bird associated with the Viking god Odin (see page 26). Many chieftains had a raven device on their flags. Earl Sigurd of Orkney's raven banner looked like the bird was flying when it fluttered in the breeze.

Berserkers

These especially ferocious Viking elite troops dedicated themselves to Odin. They wore bearskins and often fought without any armour. Bloodthirsty berserkers worked themselves into a frenzy of excitement before a battle so that they would feel no pain.

Shield wall

This battle tactic was used when facing an advancing enemy. Warriors in the front few ranks of the Viking forces overlapped their shields, forming a solid wall. The warriors stuck their spears through the small gaps between the shields. This made it very hard for attackers to break the shield wall without being killed.

◀ These replica shields are decorated with ravens. Warriors would have overlapped their shields in battle to create a shield wall.

IF YOU WERE A VIKING WARRIOR...

You might have to help capture a walled town. Carrying your sword or axe, and heavy wooden shield, you'd have to struggle up a long ladder to the top of the walls where a bloody fight awaited. Defenders on top of the walls would be throwing heavy rocks and boiling water at you, or trying to push your ladder over with long poles.

▲ A walled town, as depicted in an Anglo-Saxon manuscript.

◄ This statue of King Alfred the Great of Wessex is in Winchester.

VIKINGS IN ENGLAND

In 865 a Danish Viking army landed in eastern England. The Vikings wanted to conquer lands ruled by the Anglo-Saxons and settle there themselves. The Viking Great Army fought its way across the country for 14 years. But eventually King Alfred the Great of Wessex defeated the Viking leader, Guthrum, in a big battle at Edington in 878. The Danes, unable to defeat Alfred, agreed to settle in the area of eastern England known as the Danelaw.

Making camp

Viking chieftains ordered their warriors to build temporary fortified camps. In Denmark, archaeologists have found the remains of four of these camps, dating from about 980. The biggest is Aggersborg, which is 240 m in diameter.

Trelleborg

Experts think the building of this Viking camp was ordered by King Harald Bluetooth when he was trying to unite Denmark into one kingdom. Trelleborg had a shallow moat and two walls made of tree trunks for protection. Inside the walls were many large buildings called

▲ An aerial view of Trelleborg showing the base of the walls, the ditch and the outlines of Viking longhouses.

longhouses. These were 30 m long and had thatched roofs. There were workshops for craft workers as well. Bones from graves outside the camp walls show that women and children lived there too.

IF YOU WERE A VIKING WARRIOR...

Inside a Viking longhouse, you'd sit and sleep on long wooden benches, with cushions or animal furs for comfort. It would be smoky, as there was a large central fireplace but no proper chimney. You'd cook your food in a large cauldron hanging over the fire. In the winter you'd eat salted or smoked meat or fish.

Repton

In 873, when the Viking Great Army was rampaging around England (see page 19), they camped for the winter at Repton, in Derbyshire. They built a defensive earth bank around their campsite and used an old Anglo-Saxon church as their headquarters. Here archaeologists have found Viking warrior burials. Experts found swords, buckles and everyday Viking objects in the graves at Repton.

FINDS

Archaeologists found many objects from Viking everyday life at Trelleborg. These included combs, necklaces made of glass beads, and gold cloak pins.

▲ This Viking warrior's sword was found at Repton.

Warriors go east

Viking warriors travelled far to the south and east of their Scandinavian homelands. Some of these journeys took them as far as the Black Sea, near what is today Turkey, and beyond.

▲ Re-enactors sail replica Viking ships up the River Volga in Russia.

Into Russia

Swedish Vikings crossed the Baltic Sea to make raiding and trading voyages deep into the heart of Russia. They navigated up rivers like the Volga to reach trading centres such as Kiev. When they could sail no further, they travelled onwards by foot, horse or camel.

Raid and trade

On their journeys, Viking warriors raided poorly defended towns for treasure and other valuables. But they also brought goods to barter (exchange) with merchants they met.

Byzantine Vikings

Some Vikings travelled across the Black Sea to attack the capital of the Byzantine Empire, Constantinople (now Istanbul). The Byzantine emperor admired their fearless fighting skills and recruited Vikings into his elite troop of bodyguards, the Varangian Guard.

Eastern evidence

In Scandinavia, archaeologists have found evidence of the Vikings' eastern travels. Experts have unearthed silver objects from Baghdad (in Iraq), metalwork from Persia (modern-day Iran) and statues from northern India.

Give and take

Viking warriors who travelled south and east were influenced by the fashions and equipment of the regions they visited. Some adopted the baggy trousers, long coats and pointy helmets of Central Asia. It's even possible that Russia takes its name from Swedish Vikings - local Slavs referred to them as the 'Rus'.

▲ Experts believe this statue of Buddha was made in Kashmir (now in India and Pakistan) in the 500s. It was found on the Swedish island of Helgo.

ERIK WAS 'ERE...

You can still see evidence of Vikings in Istanbul today. Hagia Sophia was once a famous place of religious worship (it is now a museum) and in one of the building's galleries you can see graffiti carved into the stonework using letters known as runes – the Viking alphabet. These were made more than 1,000 years ago.

▼ Vikings scratched these runes into the stonework of Hagia Sophia.

Warriors go west

While some Vikings were raiding and trading in the lands to the south and east of Scandinavia, others were setting off westwards on epic journeys of exploration.

Heading west

Viking raids on England (see pages 8-9) were quickly followed by attacks on Scotland, Ireland, France, Germany and the Netherlands. Once an area had been conquered, settlements and colonies eventually followed. The region of Normandy in France is so named because Vikings (the 'north-men') settled there.

Scotland and beyond

In the 800s Norwegian Vikings came across a big island they named 'Snaeland' (land of snow) - today's Iceland. After surviving a very hard winter, the Vikings were amazed to see the land turn green when summer came. Viking settlers soon followed, and within 60 years Iceland was fully populated.

Onwards

In about 980, a Viking called Erik the Red sailed west from Iceland and discovered an uninhabited land with an even more extreme climate. He settled on the coast and named the land 'Greenland' in order to attract other settlers.

These traditional Viking houses in Iceland are roofed with turf to keep them warm in winter and cool in summer. ▼

IF YOU WERE A VIKING WARRIOR...

Had you settled in Greenland you would have had to scrape a living in the harsh Arctic climate. You would have hunted walruses for their hide and ivory, and seals for their meat and blubber (fat). Your family would have raised sheep and cattle on the few areas of farmland along the coast. You would have been totally dependent on Iceland and Norway for iron tools and wood.

Sheep in Greenland need to be very hardy to survive the harsh winters. ▶

Icelandic stories say that 25 ships full of settlers left Iceland in 985 bound for Greenland, but that only 14 ships survived the harsh and dangerous voyage.

An aerial view of the reconstructed Viking settlement at L'Anse aux Meadows in Newfoundland. ▼

DISCOVERING NORTH AMERICA

Erik the Red's son, Leif Erikson, discovered Vinland – today's Newfoundland, in Canada – in about 1000. A small settlement was founded there at a place today called L'Anse aux Meadows. Here in the 1960s, archaeologists discovered the remains of Viking longhouses and wooden objects. It seems the settlement was abandoned within a few years.

Valhalla and the afterlife

As followers of a pagan religion, Vikings believed in many gods. Two - Odin and Thor - were especially important to warriors.

Odin

This important deity was the god of the dead. Viking warriors feared and respected Odin because they believed he could grant victory or defeat in battle.

Thor

Thor was the god of the sky and of thunder. Thor had a powerful magic hammer called Mjöllnir. With this he protected Asgard, the place where the gods lived. Many Viking warriors wore a lucky amulet (charm) in the shape of Thor's hammer.

Valhalla

Vikings believed that warriors killed in battle went straight to Valhalla, the huge feasting hall of Odin. Here they were welcomed with drinking horns full of mead - an alcoholic drink made from fermented honey. The warriors then feasted through the night with Odin.

▲ This Viking gravestone shows Odin riding the eight-legged horse, Sleipnir.

The Valkyrie

In early Viking stories these fierce warrior women were spirits who helped Odin. Later tales describe them as wearing armour and riding their spirit horses through the air over land and sea. Vikings believed the Valkyrie flew over battlefields to choose which of the dead they would take to Odin in Valhalla.

Ship burials

Viking chieftains were sometimes buried in a longship, surrounded by their possessions. These could include slaves, horses, weapons and armour. Vikings believed that the dead leader needed

▲ A replica Viking ship is set alight at the Viking festival of Up Helly Aa on Shetland.

all these things in the afterlife. Sometimes the ship was set on fire so that the chieftain went quickly to paradise.

THE OSEBERG SHIP

The Oseberg ship is one of the best-preserved Viking ship burials. Some experts think it is the most amazing single artefact to have survived from the Viking Age. Discovered in Norway in 1904, the ship is over 21 m long and is made of oak. Parts of it are very finely carved.

◄ The Oseberg ship on display.

Warriors become Christian

From the mid 950s onwards, Viking nations began to leave their old religious beliefs behind and become Christian. They worshipped the Christian God in churches they once would have plundered.

Kings lead the way

The spread of Christianity to faraway Scandinavia took longer than it did to other parts of Europe. Viking raiders experienced contact with Christians during their raids, so they knew of their religion. In time Christian missionaries travelled to Viking lands. Some Viking kings converted because they wanted to form alliances with Christian leaders.

Once Viking kings converted, their people quickly followed. Danish king, Harald Bluetooth, became a Christian in the 960s, followed by King Olaf Haraldsson of Norway in the mid 1020s. Ordinary Vikings began to realise that their old gods wouldn't punish them for becoming Christian, so many more people converted.

▼ The Jelling Stone, with its Viking-looking depiction of Christ.

JELLING STONE

This stone shows the earliest-known picture of Christ in Scandinavia. It was ordered to be put up by King Harald Bluetooth of Denmark in the 900s as a memorial to his parents.

▲ This typical, wooden stave church in Hopperstad, Norway, is believed to have been built around 1130.

Guthrum converts

After King Alfred the Great of Wessex defeated the Viking leader Guthrum at the Battle of Edington in 878, Guthrum agreed to convert to Christianity. He was baptised, with Alfred acting as godfather.

Stave churches

Early Christian churches built in Viking lands were made in a distinctive style. They are called stave churches because the walls were made from split tree trunks, or staves. The buildings often had elaborate Viking carvings.

Belt and braces

Some Vikings converted to Christianity but secretly held onto their old beliefs as well. Viking depictions of Jesus Christ are often strong and vigorous, in the style of old Viking gods.

This hammer of Thor pendant also has a Christian cross on it. ▶

The end of the Viking era

As time passed, Vikings who had settled in Normandy (see page 24-25) became Christian and learned to speak French. They adopted the arms and armour of Western Europe, fighting on horseback and using long, kite-shaped shields. In 1066 Duke William of Normandy, a descendant of the Viking, Rollo, led the Norman invasion of England. His forces defeated the army of the ruling Anglo-Saxons at the Battle of Hastings and William 'the Conqueror' became king of England.

Glossary

Anglo-Saxons The people who lived in England at the time Vikings began to raid.

Archaeologist An expert who unearths objects from the past and works out their meaning.

Artefact An object from the past.

Baptise To welcome someone into the Christian faith.

Bloodthirsty Violent.

Byzantine Empire An empire in the eastern Mediterranean area that existed from CE 330 to 1453.

Cauldron A large metal cooking pot.

Christian Someone who believes that Jesus Christ is the son of God.

Colony A settlement in a faraway place.

Conquered Defeated by an invading army.

Convert To change religion.

Device A graphic symbol carried by a leader as a means of identification.

Duel An armed fight between two people.

Epic Far ranging, long, difficult or amazing.

Estuary The wide mouth of a river.

Exotic To do with a faraway place.

Feud A long-standing row between families or peoples.

Flex To twist and bend without breaking.

Fortified A place surrounded by walls and ditches for security.

Furnace A very hot fireplace used to create molten metal.

Godfather At a baptism, a man who promises to be a religious guide for the person being baptised.

Hull The body of a boat or ship.

Merchants People who make money buying and selling goods.

Missionary Someone sent out by a church to spread their faith.

Monastery A religious building where monks live together.

Monk A religious person who spends their life praying and working in a monastery.

Mythical Having to do with myths - tales of gods and monsters.

Navigate To find the way.

Pagan Believing in many gods.

Retainers Servants or warriors who look after and defend a leader.

Ruthless Single-minded and without mercy.

Shaft A long piece of wood used as the handle of a weapon, or the main part of an arrow.

Tarred Something covered with a sticky substance that makes it waterproof.

Some Viking websites

www.bbc.co.uk/education/topics/ztyr9j6
The BBC's primary history section on Vikings and Viking life.

www.jorvik-viking-centre-co.uk
Explore this important Viking site and visitor attraction in York.

www.museumoflondon.co.uk
The Museum of London records the history of London, and its collections include Vikings artefacts found in the River Thames.

www.en.natmus.dk/museums/trelleborg/visit-trelleborg/
Information on Trelleborg Viking fortress from the National Museums of Denmark.

Note to parents and teachers: Every effort has been made by the Publishers to ensure that the websites in this book are suitable for children, that they are of the highest educational value, and that they contain no inappropriate or offensive material. However, because of the nature of the Internet, it is impossible to guarantee that the contents of these sites will not be altered. We strongly advise that Internet access is supervised by a responsible adult.

Timeline

CE 793 First Viking raid at Lindisfarne on the north-east coast of England

799 First Viking raids on France

800 Vikings land in Orkney, Shetland and the Faroe Islands

810 Vikings raid present-day Netherlands and northern Germany

860 Vikings trade in Russia and reach Constantinople in Turkey

866 Viking army invades England, looking for land to settle

867 Vikings capture York and rebuild it as Jorvik

870 Vikings discover Iceland and begin to settle there

878 Anglo-Saxon King Alfred the Great of Wessex defeats Viking leader Guthrum at the Battle of Edington

911 Vikings begin to settle in Normandy

960 King Harald Bluetooth of Denmark converts to Christianity

982 Vikings discover Greenland

986 Vikings discover North America

995 King Olaf of Norway converts to Christianity

1001 Vikings founded a short-lived colony in Newfoundland

1066 Norman Duke William is victorious over Anglo-Saxon forces at the Battle of Hastings. William becomes king of England

1100 End of the Viking Age

Index